Charles Stewart Loch

Charity Organisation

Charles Stewart Loch

Charity Organisation

ISBN/EAN: 9783743330429

Manufactured in Europe, USA, Canada, Australia, Japa

Cover: Foto ©ninafisch / pixelio.de

Manufactured and distributed by brebook publishing software (www.brebook.com)

Charles Stewart Loch

Charity Organisation

CHARITY ORGANISATION

BY

C. S. LOCH, B.A.

SECRETARY TO THE LONDON CHARITY ORGANISATION SOCIETY

LONDON
SWAN SONNENSCHEIN & CO
PATERNOSTER SQUARE
1890

SOCIAL SCIENCE SERIES.

EACH 2s. 6d.

1. **WORK AND WAGES**
   Professor THOROLD ROGERS.
2. **CIVILISATION: ITS CAUSE AND CURE**
   EDWARD CARPENTER.
3. **THE QUINTESSENCE OF SOCIALISM**
   DR. SCHÄFFLE.
   "Precisely the manual needed. Brief, lucid, fair and wise."—*British Weekly.*
4. **DARWINISM AND POLITICS**
   D. G. RITCHIE, M.A.
5. **THE RELIGION OF SOCIALISM**
   E. BELFORT BAX.
6. **ETHICS OF SOCIALISM**
   E. BELFORT BAX.
7. **THE DRINK QUESTION.**
   DR. KATE MITCHELL.
8. **PROMOTION OF GENERAL HAPPINESS**
   Professor MICHAEL MACMILLAN.
9. **ENGLAND'S IDEAL**
   EDWARD CARPENTER.
10. **SOCIALISM IN ENGLAND**
    SIDNEY WEBB, LL.B.
11. **BISMARCK AND STATE SOCIALISM**
    W. H. DAWSON.
12. **GODWIN'S POLITICAL JUSTICE (On Property)**
    Edited by H. S. SALT
13. **THE FRENCH REVOLUTION**
    E. BELFORT BAX.
14. **CHARITY ORGANISATION**
    C. S. LOCH, *Secy. Charity Organ. Soc.*
15. **CRIME AND THE PRISON SYSTEM**
    W. DOUGLAS MORRISON, *of H.M. Gaol, Wandsworth.*

LONDON: SWAN SONNENSCHEIN & CO., PATERNOSTER SQUARE.

PREFACE.

THIS little book is the reprint of a paper entitled *De l'Organisation de l'Assistance*, written for the *Congrès International d'Assistance*, held in Paris in July and August, 1889. My wish was to give such a sketch of Charity Organisation as would indicate not merely the methods and plan of the Charity Organisation Society, but would enable the readers to form some conception of the social and other conditions under which, alone, in my opinion, an organisation of charity can take deep root and develop. I wished also to state some of the principles of the administration of relief, not arbitrarily, but as they have been worked out by English experience. In doing this I may appear to have written with too little detail for a book, and yet with too great detail and with a reference to too many general questions, for a paper. But one consideration determined me. My readers were to be persons of other countries, not specially acquainted with English life and thought. It was necessary, therefore, not merely to describe the plant, "Charity Organisation," but to give some particulars of its habitat also. If our English methods were to be of use to others than ourselves, it was not enough to define them. Only if the social conditions under which they could be acclimatised were set forth, could the reader judge whether they, or any part of them, could be transplanted or adapted. One prevalent fallacy in many statements in regard to social matters in other countries is to portray this or that social plan or movement, to consider it by itself and isolated from other social conditions, and to jump to the conclusion that it is likely to be advantageous to us, because it is of use to others.

Another point I should mention. I have attempted in this paper to deal with the Charity Organisation movement as a whole. This had not been done before, but it appeared to me to be justified by the progress of the movement in the last twenty years. I can only regret that limits of space obliged me to make little or no use of a great mass of evidence which was kindly furnished to me, particularly by some of the Charity Organisation Societies in England and Scotland.

On a few points I have revised the paper for republication, but I have thought it best to leave the figures for 1888, the latest at the time available, as they stood.

After all, I fear that, as my paper appears in a scientific series, a more elaborate and complete treatment of the subject than I have been able to give, may be expected by the reader. Had time and opportunity permitted, I should willingly have undertaken such a task. Now, I can only hope that, limited though it be in many directions, it may at least prove suggestive to those who are in any way interested in the questions on which it touches.

C. S. L.

May, 1890.

CONTENTS.

		Page
I. Charity Organisation a New Movement	. . .	1

II. The Lesson of the Poor Law—
    (1) The English Poor Law 10
    (2) The Effect on Pauperism of Poor Law Relief provided to meet ordinary contingencies . . . 18
    (3) Relief to the able-bodied, considered as relief to meet ordinary contingencies 23
    (4) Out-door Relief, considered as relief given to meet ordinary contingencies 25
    (5) The Organisation of Charity and the Individual System 33

III. Principles and Methods of Charitable Relief—
    (1) The need of Charity Organisation 36
    (2) Charity Organisation Societies 48
    (3) Inquiry 61
    (4) The Almoner 77
    (5) Relief 85
    (6) Co-operation 89
    (7) General Methods 96
    (8) Objections to Charity Organisation 97

ERRATUM.

Page 103. Line 16. *Dele* "slow but' and the sentence following.
          Line 20. *For* £6,871,807. *Read* £17,780,006.

CHARITY ORGANISATION.

I. CHARITY ORGANISATION AS A NEW MOVEMENT.

CHARITY ORGANISATION represents a new movement of thought and social reform in England. The Charity Organisation Society was established in 1869, and in the department of social life, in which its work lies, progress is necessarily and rightly slow. Even now, therefore, after the lapse of twenty years, it seems to be too soon to sum up its aims and efforts.

A new movement in a community is the expression and recognition of some want which may have been felt before, but which has, nevertheless, been considered of secondary importance, and has found no place in the institutions of the country. Indeed, to a past generation it may have seemed impossible or even undesirable to satisfy it. But public opinion changes. The new generation comes to the front with a theory of life and duty different from that of its predecessors. Enthusiasm and energy take a new line; and the set practices and the institutions which possess the field are bent and brushed aside to give way to the new comers. There is resistance, remonstrance, and disapproval on the part of some; on the part of others kindly greeting and hopefulness; and if the intruders have opinions which are the just expression of a real want, suggest a higher ideal, and appeal to the better nature of their comrades—and if they have the courage of their opinions—they sooner or later make their influence felt. In so far as they are clear-sighted and reasonable, brave and steadfast of purpose, they succeed. They help to build up the manhood of their country.

With some hesitation, and with all respect for good men and women who may differ from us, we would claim for Charity Organisation the faith and the hopes of a new movement.

The want to which the Society gives expression, is the want of a better social and charitable relation between members of the same community. Changes in our social and political organisation have given a sharply defined reality to this want. Instead of indifference or vague regret in regard to it, we feel it keenly. We are intent on finding the causes of our failure in this respect, and on removing those causes, in some degree at least, by well-devised action, both in association with others and individually. What has intensified our feeling of this want, and transformed it (to use the old phrase) into "a hunger and thirst?."

Our conception of the duty of the State to its citizens, and of the citizens to the State, and of the duty of the rich to the poor, differs greatly from that generally held in times past. In the old Greek days, for instance, the artizans and labourers were, as a rule, outside the pale of citizenship. They had no vote. They were the workers of the community, its slave-bees, generally expected to be of a "mean and rascally" nature. They were not supposed to have sufficient education or wisdom to take part in the government. *Mutatis mutandis*, this theory of the position of the lower classes would apply to feudal times and to some countries in our own day. But now the world in general has grown democratic. The great mass of adult male persons are voters. There is to be, politically at least, no dependent class, and all are to share in the government. With this change there is, or should be, a change in the methods of administration in many departments—amongst others, in those departments which concern the lives of the poor. It is more than ever the interest of the State to prevent the existence of a class so poor as to be on the verge of dependence, or actually in receipt of poor relief. Pauperism is the social enemy of the modern State. The State wants citizens. It cannot afford to have any outcast or excluded classes, citizens that are not citizens. All are citizens in name; it must see that they are so in reality. It must do its utmost to change the dependent sections of the community into independent. It cannot be content with the chronic indigence and social feebleness of any great mass of citizens—with paupers, who are paupers indeed, whether they be classified as such in public returns or are the habitual recipients of the casual bounty of the rich and of charitable institutions. Accordingly it becomes a duty of the State by some means to prevent pauperism, and of citizens to give their service to the State for that purpose.

Also, in the relations of the richer to the poorer members of the community, new or forgotten duties are brought to light. Of late years throughout the length and breadth of the land there has been constant complaint of the hardness of the conditions of labour. Reforms have been agitated for an eight hours' day, for the provision of better dwellings for the artizan and labouring classes, for some artificial equalisation of incomes, for the abolition of private ownership in land, and so forth. Experiments have been made and legal enactments proposed to accomplish some of these ends, and popular discussion seems to have found a chief interest in philanthropic methods of reforming society. Considered in its true bearings, this constantly repeated plea of the labourer is a demand for a fuller and completer life; and the constant discussion of it represents on the other side, if not an acceptance of the demand, at least a willing attention to it. Suppose the demand be even partially accepted, not as on behalf of the State or on economic grounds, but on behalf of individuals and on moral grounds, and we have the recognition of the new and forgotten duties to which I have referred. It follows that, in the administration of private or charitable relief, there must be a change. Private service in a great measure takes the place of private relief.

Gifts of money, doles of food and clothing cannot be the sole and simple expression of the charity of the rich or of those who are better furnished than their neighbours with this world's good things. Such gifts, in the main, are for dependents, whom it seems hopeless to try and raise up, or for members of classes that are expected to remain dependent, and to find some solace for the hardships of life in the petty presents and patronage of their superiors. The new charity requires of the rich that, for the common good, they submit to the common yoke of labour, and that they help the poor to become self-dependent and competent fellow-citizens. And, if gifts there be, it requires that the gift should be the least token of the sympathy that prompts it, and that devotion, intelligence, and common sense should use the gift, so that it influence and elevate character. The new charity does not seek material ends, but to create a better social and individual life.

I have referred to Charity Organisation as giving some expression to a new sense of duty on the part of citizens and individuals. To complete the sketch, I should make some reference to the position of religious communities in this matter. They represent a third party. Seldom do they throw themselves heartily into the work of the State. They leave it rather to private interest or ambition to force a way and find a duty there. They seldom preach a gospel of noble citizenship. And in regard to individuals, they have given prominence rather to the obligation of accepting certain religious views than to that of acting up to a continually completer ideal of duty. But let honour be paid, where honour is so clearly due. From among the ardent members of religious communities have come the chief apostles of charity to the afflicted, the sick, the fallen, and the distressed. They had an almost pitiless disregard of claims and duties, which we cannot ignore; but they were fearless in their sympathies, and so intent upon their mission, that they felt that nothing ought to hinder them from sharing in the sorrows and miseries of the very poorest of mankind. Yet their efforts to improve the general conditions of the life of the poor were often but feeble and transient. Their charity was not allied to any wider conception of citizenship. It was too often, perhaps, the hopeless push and protest of the saint against the evils of a hopeless world, where he had no abiding place; and then, if zeal grew cold, it found a sufficient expression in a charity from which love had evaporated, and which was no better than the payment of a toll on the high road of life. Now, it may be, the religious consciousness is slowly changing, and the "love of the neighbour whom we have seen" is becoming more truthful and more real. If this be so, alms will no longer be used to further religious teaching, or gain acceptance of religious views; the petty charity of doles and food and clothing will give place to a charity which is the outward sign of that sense of membership in one common life, into which, according to the Christian ideal, the whole community should be drawn. Here and now will be found a life eternal. If between the religious spirit, and the sense of duty in matters which concern the citizen and the individual, there were an alliance, a combined effort might be made to prevent pauperism, with a fervour and directness of purpose, that might well be invincible. Citizenship would shape the general measures and fix the duties of members of the community; and the religious spirit would give the devotion that would make the individual long suffering and persistent in the endeavour to help his neighbour.

These three forces then are at work. A sense of citizenship is making new claims on the individual. The individual is pressed by other members of the community to recognise new or forgotten duties. The religious consciousness of the community is deepening. These facts represent the conditions under which charity organisation can exist, find scope for the new element that it brings to bear on social problems, and fulfil its purpose. If it has any lasting influence, any real existence, it is due to this; that it is charity—an enthusiasm, as of religion, for the common good, and that, as such, it strives to ennoble citizenship and to perfect it, and, for the relief and prevention of distress, endeavours to realise the duties of individual to individual, and to promote the fulfilment of these duties by co-operation.

II. THE LESSON OF THE POOR LAW.

(1.) *The English Poor Law.*

THE end of charity is to prevent pauperism. Many causes go to make pauperism. There are many duties of citizenship which tend to prevent it. We have, however, to deal more particularly with those that concern the administration of relief, whether public or private. Relief, as it is now administered, often produces pauperism. Under what conditions may it have the opposite effect? Our answer is, that it must be organised. By this we mean that it must be administered on some common principles and methods. What are these common principles and methods?

One I have already touched upon. We should help the poor to become self-dependent and competent citizens. We take it that the family is the civic unit. A sweet and wholesome family life is the first condition of good citizenship. The head of the family must be responsible for providing against all the ordinary contingencies of life, for himself, his wife and his children. However it be set aside in the pressure of existence, this is the accepted legal position. If it be not accepted and acted upon, the family will live under no strong and sturdy roof-tree, but, whatever relief may be forthcoming, they will be liable to constant starvation and misery. The main prop of family life will be wanting—the continuous provision of the necessaries of existence. That the head of the family should provide against the ordinary conditions of life is the condition of self-preservation in a civilised community. In other words, care and foresight in the use of wages and property is to the family in civic life what quickness of sense and strength are to the brute in the competition of wild beasts. If this care and foresight be present, there is at least the foundation of a progressive family life ; if it be not present, the very pressure of the ordinary needs of life will reduce the family to incompetence, weakness, and savagery. Thus, rightly considered, the economic basis is a moral basis.

But poverty is a relative term. Self-sustaining poverty, from the point of view of relief, may very well be left to look after itself. Provided that laws for the general well-being of the citizen, such, for instance, as sanitary laws, are enforced, and that no hindrances are put in the way of thrift, the less it is meddled with the better. Out of the services which half the world is ready to give, by way of amusing, edifying, or converting the other half, it will choose for itself what it finds best. We should be anxious neither by State provision nor voluntary charities to tempt it to depend on others. Our business should not be with the poor as such, but with those who are in distress or destitution or who have in them the seeds of pauperism.

In the first place, then, we have to consider and deal with those whose distress is due to a disregard of the ordinary contingencies of life. Distress of this kind is clearly more or less preventible. Other distress there is, which cannot be foreseen, and which may well call for relief, especially on the ground that it is not preventible.

It is hardly too much to say that our administrators, whether public or private, have not as a rule accepted this distinction as to the causes of distress and acted upon it. Relief, generally speaking, has not been administered so as to prevent pauperism.

In so far as the principles and methods of

relief are common to the administration of both public and private funds, I have referred to both in this paper. But before discussing this question, it is necessary to sketch in outline our English Poor Law System, and to describe the position taken by Charity Organisation Societies. The one depends on the other.

In England, the administration of public relief is in the hands of Poor Law Guardians, who are elected annually, or in some instances triennially to the office. The area of election and administration is the Parish or combination of Parishes—called a Union. A Central Board—the Local Government Board—supervises the whole system, and relief is administered in accordance with its "orders." There are two main forms of relief—in-door relief, and out-door relief. In the granting of the latter the Guardians have considerable discretion. "The fundamental principle with respect to the legal relief of the poor," write the Poor Law Commissioners in 1839, "is that the condition of the pauper ought to be on the whole less eligible than that of the independent labourer. The equity and expediency of this principle are equally obvious. Unless the condition of the pauper is on the whole less eligible than that of the independent labourer, the law destroys the strongest motives to good conduct, steady industry, providence, and frugality among the labouring classes, and induces persons, by idleness and imposture, to throw themselves upon the poor rates for support. The pauper has no just ground of complaint, if at the same time that his physical wants are amply provided for, his condition should be less eligible than that of the poorest class of those who contribute to his support."

In the service of the Guardians there is for the management of general business a Clerk, and for the administration of out-door relief Medical Officers, and Relieving Officers, who in the larger Unions have each a section of the district under their charge. Cases of sickness are referred to the Medical Officer, and in London there are Poor Law Dispensaries for the treatment of the sick, who receive, what we call, medical orders. It is the duty of the Relieving Officer " to receive all applications for relief made to him within his district, and forthwith examine into the circumstances of every case by visiting the house of the applicant (if situated within his district), and by making all necessary inquiries into the state of health, the ability to work, the condition and family and the means of such applicant, and to report the result of such inquiries to the Guardians at their next ordinary meeting." He also distributes the relief to those to whom the Guardians decide to give it. Further, "in every case of sudden and urgent necessity," he has to afford " such relief as may be requisite." He is thus in a very responsible position. He "has no absolute discretion in deciding what is a case of urgent necessity;" and he is personally responsible if evil result from his refusal. It will be seen from this that the claim for relief on the part of the applicant is very fully recognised. It is a claim under the pressure of which, most honorary officers would shrink from the responsibility of acting as almoners. We have thus a very absolute legal system of relief in force in England, with a paid Relieving Officer to make inquiries and give relief on behalf of the Board of Guardians.

With regard to the administration of out-door relief there are some restrictions. It cannot be given to establish an applicant in trade or business; to redeem tools, implements, or other articles from pawn; or to purchase or give such articles, unless they be clothing or bedding where urgently needed, food, fuel, or articles of absolute necessity. Able-bodied men are either relieved only in the Workhouse, or, if out of the House, they are set to work, and half the relief which they receive must be in food, fuel, or other articles of absolute necessity. Thus outdoor relief—indeed all Poor Law relief—is intended to supply merely the necessities of life; and as a corollary to this, it is intended for the destitute and the destitute only.

Reference has been made to the Workhouse. Relief in the Workhouse, the Infirmary, or in a Poor Law School is in-door relief. It was intended by the framers of our modern Poor Law, that in-door relief, as the less eligible form of assistance, should be the rule, out-door relief the exception. If any of those present should wish to see what an English Workhouse, Infirmary, or District School are like, he will find careful plans of these in the English Economic Section of this Exhibition.[1] In the Workhouse there is a classification of inmates, more or less complete.

[1] These plans, with reports and books bearing on the question of the administration of relief, were collected for the Paris Exhibition of 1889.

Work is provided, but the inmates are often old, often incompetent, and the Workhouse is usually of little or no service at present for work, furnished with a view to reforming the workmen or workwomen employed within its walls; indeed, it is not likely that even with the best intentions much can be done in this direction through the agency of a Poor Law. The Workhouse is under the charge of a Master and Matron with Assistants. The Infirmary, which is under the charge of a Medical Officer, has now developed, in many instances, into a very complete Hospital. The District or Poor Law Schools are often very large—too large, many critics say. And besides the institutions I have mentioned, there are Casual Wards for wayfarers and vagrants. These are now built, very frequently, on the " separate system," that is, on a plan by which there is assigned to each inmate a separate cell. On admission he has to take a bath; before leaving he has to do a task of work.

There is thus a great array of Poor Law Institutions erected and managed at considerable cost. The relief, which is at their disposal, is for the destitute; and the destitute may be

B

considered to have a very stringent claim upon it. The system is in the main deterrent, rather than reformatory. It recognises the poor as a class who are in general to be left alone and not to be interfered with by the administrators of public relief. It has to deal with those only who become paupers. It affords, what I may call, a background for the organisation of charitable relief. To ignore it would be foolish. To utilise and improve it, according to the lines of its development, is a first duty with those who would organise charity. To relieve on methods that will not pauperise those who are in distress and cannot or should not be relieved by the Poor Law, is their task. It follows that charity organisation will promote co-operation between the administrators of Poor Law or Public relief and the administrators of charitable funds, so that each body by a division of labour may fulfil its own function.

(2.) *The effect on Pauperism of Poor Law Relief provided to meet ordinary contingencies.*

Now to return to the question of distress due to a disregard of the ordinary contingencies of life. The distribution of relief in order to meet the ordinary contingencies of life tends to increase pauperism. This conclusion applies to Poor Law relief and charitable relief alike. In the case of Poor Law relief, the refusal of relief except on unpalatable conditions throws the individual on his own resources, in a manner advantageous to himself and to the community. In the case of charity, to meet the ordinary contingencies of life by relief is hardly less harmful than in the case of the Poor Law, unless it be combined with the exercise of such influence on the part of the donor as will induce the person to provide for himself against similar contingencies in the future. We will take the Poor Law first, and note the effects of an administration, which has gradually become more strict—in regard to pauperism in general, in regard to able-bodied paupers, and in regard particularly to out-door relief.

The demand for relief is usually highest in January. I choose that month therefore.[1] Taking the four years 1857, 1867, 1877, and 1887, we have the following results as regards England and Wales and the Metropolis :—

[1] Seventeenth Annual Report of the Local Government Board—1887-8, see pp. 213, 214, 215, 220, and 226.

England and Wales.

Year.	Estimated Population.	Numbers of Paupers relieved on last day of 5th week of January.			Number of Paupers in every 1000 Inhabitants.
		In-door.	Out-door.	Total.	
1857	19,042,412	138,863	781,745	920,608	48·3
1867	21,409,684	150,920	872,631	1,023,551	47·8
1877	24,370,267	153,846	532,824	686,670	28·2
1887	27,870,586	195,864	583,097	778,961	27·9
The Metropolis.					
1857	2,591,815	30,736	90,541	121,277	46·8
1867	3,040,761	34,811	134,088	168,899	55·5
1877	3,489,428	39,449	46,656	86,105	24·7
1887	4,149,533	58,957	46,242	105,199	25·4

The years 1867, 1868, 1869, 1870 and 1871 may be taken as bad years. There was much distress. The shipbuilding trade was leaving the London Docks for the North; there was cholera in 1867; in 1869 there was a very severe winter. In these years the number of paupers per thousand of the population was in England and Wales, 47·8, 48·1, 46·5, 47·5, 47·4;

in the Metropolis, 55·5, 53·5, 49·2, 52·3, 50·4. Then the figures dropped. But during that time the necessity of adopting some principle of the administration of relief was forcing itself upon the attention of many men. Pauperism seemed to be growing apace. Relief was abundant, but misery and destitution seemed to increase in spite of it, seemed almost to feed and multiply upon it. Many thoughts and endeavours at length found a practical result in the establishment of the Charity Organisation Society. Till 1877 and 1878, there were better times; but the administration of the Poor Law was made more strict. It was felt that Poor Law relief must be considered in the light of municipal relief of the destitute rather than municipal charity to the poor. One or two East End Unions began to reduce their out-door relief. The need of co-operation between the administrators of public or Poor Law, and of private or charitable funds was recognised. "Too many cooks were spoiling the broth." Organisation was indispensable; and Mr. Goschen, at that time President of the Local Government Board, issued in 1869 his Poor Law Minute on Co-operation between the Poor Law and Charity.

He pointed out that charity might, at least, co-operate with the Poor Law in regard to the supply in suitable cases of those forms of help, which under the Out-door Relief Orders (see above) were expressly forbidden. The new ideas gradually prevailed among, at least, a certain number of persons who took an active part in the administration of both public and private relief. The result was seen in the years 1879, 1880, 1881, 1882, when there was much depression of trade. In those years the rate of paupers per thousand of the population in England and Wales rose from 28·2 in 1877, to 31·6 in 1879; 31·4 in 1880; 31·3 in 1881; and in 1882 it fell again to 28·8. But in the Metropolis the figures were less. The rate of paupers per thousand of the population was 24·7, 25·4, 27·3, 28·0, 25·6. The rate, it is evident, is in some cases less than half that of the previous series of bad years. Between 1867 and 1871 the Metropolis was more pauperised than the country at large. Between 1879 and 1882 it was found to be less so. In 1885, 1886 and 1887, there was much complaint of want of work. Yet the increase of pauperism was not great, in spite of the fact that, contrary to the judgment of many of the newer generation of administrators, a Mansion House Fund was opened in 1885 and £78,000 were contributed to it. At the time when this was done there was little short of a panic. For a week or more the relief was almost thrown away, so fast and furiously was it shovelled out. But by degrees better counsels prevailed, and the utmost was done to adhere to sound principles. In 1887 the ratio of paupers per thousand of the population was in the country 27·9; in the Metropolis 25·4.

(3.) *Relief to the able-bodied—considered as relief to meet ordinary contingencies.*

Another test of special importance in view of the line of argument adopted in this paper is the number of adult able-bodied paupers who receive relief.

The following figures refer to England and Wales :—

Year ending Lady Day.	Mean Number of Adult Able-bodied In-door Paupers, excluding Vagrants.	Rated per 1000 of Population.	Mean Number of Adult Able-bodied Out-door Paupers, excluding Vagrants.	Rated per 1000 of Population.	Mean Number of Adult Able-bodied Paupers (In-door & Out-door), excluding Vagrants.	Rated per 1000 of Population.
1849	26,558	1·5	202,265	11·7	228,823	13·2
1857	19,660	1·0	120,415	6·3	140,075	7·4
1867	19,740	0·9	128,685	6·0	148,425	6·9
1877	16,446	0·7	72,952	3·0	89,398	3·7
1887	23,002	0·8	79,560	2·9	102,562	3·7

Similar figures for the Metropolis are as follows :—

1862[1]	4,466	1·6	14,355	5·1	18,821	6·7
1867	4,259	1·4	19,433	6·4	23,692	7·8
1877	4,002	1·1	7,827	2·2	11,829	3·3
1887	5,415	1·3	6,921	1·7	12,336	3·0
1888	5,935	1·4	7,525	1·8	13,460	3·2

If the series of Returns as to England and Wales, from which the above figures are taken, be examined, it appears that able-bodied pauperism rose, at the time of the Cotton Famine

[1] The first year available.

in 1863, to 10·9 per thousand of the population, but even then it was less than it was in 1849. It rose again in 1867, 1868, 1869, 1870, reaching its highest figure in 7·9 per thousand of the population. In the bad years of the present decade it reached in 1880 its highest figure, 4·6 per thousand.

In the Metropolis able-bodied pauperism rose to 9·8 per thousand in 1869, 10·2 in 1870, falling to 10·0 per thousand in 1871; and the bad years of the present decade have not raised it above 3·3. This was in 1880. If we compare the figures for 1862 with those for 1888, we shall see that while the numbers of able-bodied paupers in receipt of in-door relief, in the face of a very large increase of population, increased only by 1,469, the numbers in receipt of out-door relief have decreased by 6,830.

(4.) *Out-door relief, considered as relief given to meet ordinary contingencies.*

Before drawing a conclusion, however, I would refer to the reduction of out-door relief. Very much of the charitable assistance that is given to the poor, is out-door relief, distributed with a view to meeting the ordinary contingencies of life. When, therefore, the effect of such relief, administered on a large scale, can be shown, it is worth while to chronicle the results. The conclusions that apply to Poor Law out-door relief will apply, *mutatis mutandis,* to charitable. In consequence of the series of Returns that have been issued year by year by our Poor Law Authorities in England, we are, I think, able to submit a more exact statement on points such as these, than could, so far as I know, be furnished for any other country.

In poor Unions the Poors Rate may be a severe tax; and apart from the bad moral and economic results of a large distribution of relief, a restriction of relief may be an important financial question to the ratepayer. At any rate in poor Unions, where the problem was a serious one financially, it was first and most successfully dealt with. With most people it is not the ultimate usefulness of their gift or of the relief which they furnish, that concerns them; the question rather is, whether they can give without serious inconvenience to themselves. In the purlieus of a rich district, accordingly, pauperism and degradation often abound.

In Whitechapel, a poor Union in the East of London, out-door relief has been practically abolished. In 1869-70 there was a hard winter. The figures in the sixth week of the first quarter of the year were: in-door paupers relieved, 1,419; out-door paupers relieved, 5,339; and the cost of out-door relief was £168 17s. 4d. per week. In the corresponding week of 1879, another hard winter, the corresponding figures were: 1,431 in-door—including 165 imbeciles at Asylums; 143 out-door—including 36 boarded-out children; and the cost of out-door relief was £91 5s. 3d. per week. In 1886, when there was a slight increase of pauperism in the Metropolis, the figures were: in-door, 1,356 (including 127 at Asylums); out-door, 63 (including 41 boarded-out children); and the weekly expenditure in out-door relief £2 10s. 11d. In the figures for 1870, imbeciles at Asylums and children boarded-out are not included.[1] Could more exact evidence be forthcoming to show how needless and inadvisable is relief provided to meet the ordinary contingencies of life?

At Stepney and St. George in the East, two other East End Unions, the same system has been adopted with similar results. Mr. A. G.

[1] See Report of Select Committee of the House of Lords (1889) on Poor Relief Evidence of Mr. Vallance, p. 498.

Crowder, a Guardian of the latter Union—the poorest in London—thus describes the change:—"They [the poor] certainly manage to get on just as well without the out-door relief dole... They have accepted the inevitable, I may almost say contentedly. I should ascribe that in a great measure to the manner in which we have adhered to our decisions. We have unflinchingly adhered to fixed rules, and we have not permitted interest or importunity to affect our action. Firmness and uniformity are essential for producing an effect on the habits of the poor. Under the old system which I saw in full work in 1875, no refusal was ever considered to be final. Applicants who were refused would go round to the Guardians and make interest with them, and the obtaining of out-door relief became, as you may call it, a perfect industry. I am sure this sort of thing goes on wherever out-door relief is given. I may also say that the ease with which this sudden reform was carried out does not appear to me to be so remarkable as at first sight it may seem, for I calculated the other day that in 1874, which was the year before the reform, the out-door relief, per pauper per week, averaged less than a shilling. I find it is much the same in Unions where out relief is [now] given. For instance, in Bethnal Green, the average amount of out-door relief, per pauper per week, only averaged 1s. 3d., and in Holborn only 1s. 5d."[1]

In Manchester, Birmingham and other towns there has also been considerable restriction of out-door relief with very good results. In country Unions where it has been tried, the results have also been remarkable. This is shown in the Bradfield Union, an agricultural Union in Hampshire.

	Pauperism exclusive of Lunatics and Vagrants.				Expenditure.		
	Paupers relieved on 1st January.			Proportion of Paupers to Population.	In Maintenance.	Out Relief.	Rate in pound of the Rateable Value.
Years.	Out-door.	In-door.	Total.	One in	£	£	@
1871	999	259	1,258	13	2,235	4,658	24½
1881	202	151	353	45	1,365	1,194	9
1888	42	100	142	126	977	305	5¾

[1] Report of Select Committee, p. 211.

In America the results have been the same. In Brooklyn, New York, U.S.A., out-door relief, chiefly through the instrumentality of Mr. Seth Low, was abolished in 1878. In 1877, 46,350 persons received out-door relief at a cost of $141,207, and 1,371 persons received in-door relief. In 1879 there was no out-door relief given at all, except coal; and the number in receipt of in-door relief was 1,389, only 18 more; in 1881 it was 1,171.[1]

So far, then, as experience may be taken as a test, we may consider that the case is proved. Relief given to meet the ordinary contingencies of life, such as out-door relief must be, is by the nature of things, inadequate. The community cannot afford to provide such relief on any sufficient scale. It must take the form of a dole, and lead to "fervid speculation"—a search for possible bounties on the part of the poor, and it will thus prove itself to be in reality no relief at all. Therefore, though the community try to help its citizens in this way, it cannot really do so, and may as well acknowledge outright the impossibility of the task. It cannot supplement

[1] See p. 14 of "Charity Organisation Societies," published by the Philadelphia Society for Organising Charity. 1881.

wages effectually; while it thinks that it is doing so, it is often, in reality, lowering the whole wage-standard for the class of labour whose earnings it supplements. On the other hand, there is positive good in the refusal of such relief. The Royal Commission on Friendly Societies reported in 1874 that—" If out-door relief could no longer be reckoned on with comparative certainty, a great stimulus would be given to exertions towards making some provision for old age. . . There is no single point in which those best acquainted with the subject more entirely concur than in recommending a more stringent administration of out-door relief as the best encouragement of providence. The adoption of this course in the Atcham Union 'had made people put money into Savings Banks with a view to laying up for old age;' and it is generally admitted that no more potent agent can be devised for inducing a man to join a Friendly Society than the dread of the Workhouse."

Speaking of the Bradfield Union, Mr. Bland-Garland writes (1888)[1] of the system of refusing out-door relief—" I can reply with perfect con-

[1] P. 10, "State Relief and other Obstacles to Thrift." Knight & Co., Fleet Street, E.C.

fidence that the condition of the people has much improved; that it never was so good as now, although wages are considerably less than they were in the earlier years of the period mentioned [about 1871-2]. They have learnt in a great measure to depend on their own exertions, to provide against a rainy day, to support their aged parents, and the demands on private charity are much less than when they were recipients of the miserable pauper dole, or were looking forward to obtaining it." He adds that "he has obtained returns of nearly all the Friendly Societies within the Union, including even the public-house clubs (the members of which have much decreased in number), and they show that the membership of the Friendly Societies has increased 148 per cent. since 1871, and that of the doctors' clubs 152 per cent."

It is quite clear, therefore, that to throw upon the citizen the duty of providing for himself and his family what is required to meet the ordinary contingencies of life, is a rule which charity may well accept; and if it does not, it is equally clear that it will not fulfil its mission of preventing pauperism by creating a better social and individual life. It will not work for good citizenship, but against it.

(5.) *The Organisation of Charity and the Individual System.*

You will see how far reaching this conclusion is. If it be right, all methods of wholesale relief, all distributions of doles, and all periodic allowances, unless in exceptional cases, should be set aside as injurious, as uncharitable. Soup kitchens, the feeding of children *en masse*, and " benevolent trading," as we have named the method much in vogue now in England of selling to the poor on a large scale, and at non-commercial rates, with the aid of charitable funds, food and other articles of necessity—all these are put equally under the ban. On the other hand, if our conclusion be adopted, the individual treatment of individual cases assumes a new importance. Charitable institutions, so far as they are necessary, find a new place in supplementing organised individual work, carried on outside their walls. Co-operation developes, because it is clear that without it charity cannot do what it would by the individual, or the family in distress. The resources at the disposal of charity have to be adapted to meet individual needs, instead of

c

being doled out on such terms as are often required by the trust deeds of old foundations: so much apiece to so many old women on a fixed day in the year, or so much as dowry on their marriage to spinsters of a certain age and good character resident in a certain place. Inquiry, careful and thorough inquiry, becomes a manifest duty, for without a sufficient knowledge of the circumstances of the individual or the family, we may not only encourage idleness and imposture, but we may fail to help those whom we most desire to make better by our relief. The standard of our personal charity, too, must be raised; we must learn how and why to help; we must be inventive in our methods, quick to influence, patient, yet decisive: we must, in fact, realise that there is an art of charity, and we must acquire it.

III. PRINCIPLES AND METHODS OF CHARITABLE RELIEF.

WE look at charitable relief, then, from a new standpoint, and have to organise the supply of it in a new way. Our conclusions are:

(1.) That for meeting the ordinary contingencies of life by way of relief, it is best that there should be no such systematic provision as will lead people to expect others to do for them, what, as citizens, they should, in the public interest, be required to do for themselves. Relief given to meet such contingencies will, unless given under the most careful restrictions and with the utmost discrimination, create pauperism.

(2.) When a request for relief of this kind is made, the question asked should be, " Ought I not to refuse?" rather than, " Ought I not to give?" And then, "If I ought to give, how can I prevent in the future the recurrence of distress due to this cause?" And the answer to that question must be the reply to another : " How can I or any one else, who will work with me, influence those who ask help, so that the distress shall not recur?" The gift avails little ; the influence may avail much. It may indeed be best to give nothing, and to rely on influence solely. And if the influence is not forthcoming, it may be best to refuse outright, for we must be true to ourselves in such a matter, and not pretend to an influence that we both lack ourselves and cannot bring others to use.

(3.) If this be true in the endeavour to persuade the thriftless to be provident, it is equally true in cases in which vice is the cause of distress. There, plainly relief by itself serves no good purpose. The evil itself must be given up; and to that end persuasion and reform with, sometimes, medical aid will be alone of service.

(4.) Lastly, there must be provision for the relief, if only for mere existence sake, of those who are incorrigible or past cure, more particularly if they have no relations able to support them. For this purpose, in regard to adults, institutions managed considerately, but in a manner that will not attract applicants, are necessary; and for the children of such adults, and for abandoned children, maintenance and education are plainly requisite, so that they, if possible, may not fall into the evil ways of their parents. It is, however, clearly to the interest of the community that institutions of these kinds should be kept within the closest limits, or they will, almost certainly, create a demand for such relief as they afford. To be idle, even under the most uncomfortable conditions, is sweeter to some than to labour.

(1.) *The Need of Charity Organisation.*

Before describing the Charity Organisation Societies, it is necessary to say a word of the kind of social world into which they have been introduced. I will in this description refer only to London.[1]

The population of the Metropolis was returned as 3,815,704 in 1881—the year of our last census. The area—about 74,688 acres—is for Poor Law purposes, divided into thirty Parishes or Unions. In eleven of these the population was less than 100,000. It was smallest in the Strand Union—33,582. In eleven it was over 150,000. It was largest in the Parish of Islington—282,865. The character of the population varies much in different districts. Some districts are suburban; in these wealthy members of the community may live "quiet and secure." They earn their bread in the city or in some thickly-populated industrial district, and their interests are divided between the district in which their business lies, and that in which their home and their pleasures are. They are probably under every temptation to ignore their duties as citizens in both places. In the business quarter, they are too busy to have time for them; in the quarter where their home is, they reside for convenience

[1] In other large towns, as is well known, the conditions are similar, though the population is smaller, and there are many minor differences.

and rest, and not to add to the toil of the day the toil of the evening. There are suburban quarters also in sections of which large numbers of artisans and labourers reside. If we pass towards the centre of the Metropolis, we find, in some districts, large numbers of better class houses, from which the better class inhabitants have migrated to more suburban parts, and which are now let in tenements to several families. We find also large areas in which there is no well-to-do class, in which the population is chiefly of one class only—clerks, artisans, or labourers. In these districts the owners of the land and houses often take very little interest in municipal affairs; nor do the men of business who live elsewhere. The management of such affairs falls into the hands of the resident tradesmen, and, to a certain extent, into those of the local clergy and doctors. Practically, the great mass of artisans, though they take part in political matters, take but little direct part in other duties of citizenship. If some suburbs be excepted, the wealth and leisure of the Metropolis may be said to be concentrated in the West End, in a district the population of which, including, however, several poor areas and spaces, may be taken at over 750,000.

In the East End there is a large industrial population; and of this quarter an elaborate analysis has recently been made by Mr. Charles Booth.[1] The population of "East London," the district which he has chosen for investigation, is 722,958; and he returns the social condition of the people according to the divisions given in the following table[2]:—

Classes according to means and position of heads of families.	Number in each class.	Percentage.
Very Poor, A. Lowest Class,	9,332	1·32
„ B. Casual earnings, ...	84,352	11·91
Poor, C. Irregular earnings,	63,506	8·96
„ D. Regular minimum,	113,728	16·05
Comfortable, E. Ordinary standard earnings, . .	314,228	44·34
Comfortable, F. Highly paid work, . . .	88,528	12·50
Well-to-do, G. Lower Middle,	23,488	3·32
„ H. Upper Middle,	11,513	1·60

By way of definition he writes :—" The divisions indicated here by ' poor" and ' very poor ' are necessarily arbitrary. By the word ' poor,' I

[1] See "Life and Labour (vol. I.) in East London." Williams & Norgate, 11 Henrietta Street, Covent Garden, London. 1889.

[2] From the above Table 14,283 inmates of institutions are excluded.

mean those who have a sufficiently regular though bare income, such as 18s. to 21s. per week for a moderate family, and by 'very poor,' those who from any cause fall much below this standard. The 'poor' are those whose means may be sufficient, but are barely sufficient, for decent, independent life; the 'very poor,' those whose means are insufficient for this, according to the usual standard of life in this country. My 'poor' may be described as living under a struggle to obtain the necessaries of life and make both ends meet; while the 'very poor' live in a state of chronic want." The area which Mr. Booth has selected contains some of the poorest parts of London; and his figures give definiteness to our problem. Here—in this area, where the problem is as serious as it is in any of the Unions of London—the "very poor" are only about 13 per cent. of the whole population. The "poor," those who are, or should be, clearly set above the line of pauperism, but may easily be tempted into pauperism, are about 25 per cent. To these the chief service that can be rendered will be the fulfilment of the duties of citizenship. Persons already in institutions, mostly in Poor-Law institutions, are not included in the above table; they number 14,283. They are either the failures of society, those who are incorrigible or past cure, or those who may be helped, as sufferers from sickness, in hospitals and infirmaries, or, as children, by education. But it should not be impossible to reduce the dependent class to very small proportions indeed, when their proportion is already comparatively small; and there must be in the large number of "comfortable" and "well-to-do" in the aggregate, such small reserves of leisure and influence as might, by a division of labour, become a great force for the improvement of the community. If this be true of so poor a quarter of London, it is still truer of almost every other district. The reform does not depend on large schemes, but on the fulfilment of duty and the use of influence in the thousand and one relations of life. Much of it will depend on raising the tone of public life in the locality. The responsibility must rest with the residents. Those in one part of London can, to a certain extent, help those in other parts; but the distance of district from district, and the difficulty of understanding the conditions of other districts without much time and study, put a limit on philanthropic energy, even when people are ready to undergo not a little exertion for the sake of doing some good.

In the centre of London is the City—the business quarter—with a very high rateable value and but few poor; but where, by a system of out-door relief, the rate of pauperism is 62·2 per thousand of the population; while in the neighbouring Union of Whitechapel, to which we have referred, it is but 16·1. Could there be a better instance to show that wealth, without discrimination and a sound sense of citizenship, is in its nature uncharitable, tends not to the social elevation, but to the degradation of the "very poor"?

Such, then, is the London into which we wish to introduce an organisation of relief, a use of public and charitable relief that shall not pauperise, but elevate the recipient and prevent pauperism.

To complete the outline, it is necessary to give some idea of the amount distributed in relief in London; and to refer shortly to the organisation of relief in connection with ecclesiastical districts and chapels.

If one may judge from officially published data and information obtainable from other sources, it would appear that the total amount spent in relief in London may be estimated as follows[1]:—

CLASS OF CHARITIES.	INCOME.	
1. City Companies	£110,000	
2. City Parochial Charities		These are likely to be utilised almost entirely for other than relief purposes, under schemes of the Charity Commissioners. In 1876 they were returned at £100,762: £40,811 for ecclesiastical, and £58,762 for secular purposes. They must now be very much more valuable.
3. Endowed Charities, Middlesex (Metropolitan, excluding the City)	39,294	
4. Endowed Charities, Surrey (Metropolitan)	23,945	
5. Endowed Charities, Kent (Metropolitan)	13,136	
6. Voluntary Parochial Charities	54,750	Estimated on Returns from a certain number of Parishes.
7. Nonconformist Churches and Chapels	32,850	Estimated.
8. Voluntary Institutions	2,183,720	Taken from Howe's Classified Directory, 1886. This *excludes* Bible, Book, and Tract Societies, Home and Foreign Missions, Church and Chapel Building Funds, Education and Apprenticeship, and other Charities not applicable for relief purposes.
9. Magistrates' Poor Boxes	3,500	
10. Charitable relief given direct		A large sum not estimated.
11. Charitable relief given in connection with Trade, Benevolent, and Friendly Societies		Not estimated.
	2,461,195	
To this may be added the cost of the total relief of the poor in connection with the Poor-Law *	2,258,029	
Total	£4,719,224	

* See Report of the Local Government Board, 1886-87, Appendix E.

[1] See "Charity Organisation Review," August, 1888.

The Voluntary Hospitals and Dispensaries in London, including Provident Dispensaries, number 160, with an expenditure estimated as being in 1887 about £723,000. The in-patients numbered about 77,000, the out-patients about 1,447,000. The total amount distributed in London in relief is thus very large, even if allowance be made for the largeness of the population; and also for the fact that a considerable portion of the relief—that connected with charitable endowments—is available only for certain fixed purposes. It must be added that while some charities are doing most useful work, others are founded on lines which are radically unsound, or are not so administered as to provide, either by themselves or in co-operation with others, the adequate assistance which is necessary to produce any permanent result. Much, also, of the money under headings 6 and 7, is given in "tickets"—orders on tradesmen for the supply of small amounts of goods, such as tea and groceries, bread, and coals, to the applicant—or temporary allowances or doles.

The Staff by whom this relief is administered is very various. In Charitable Institutions much depends on the Manager or Secretary and on the activity of a more or less active Committee. In the richer and suburban quarters there are often large numbers of District Visitors attached to the churches, and often there are many visitors connected with large and influential chapels. There are "Missions" in some of the poor parts of the town; these are supported by a church or churches or a chapel in a well-to-do district, and sometimes a large number of "Workers" take part in the administration of relief, which forms part of the Mission work. In other parishes "Sisters" have settled, and the parish relief is in their hands. In some parishes the relief is in the hands of "Deaconesses." In many there are nurses, either parochial or attached to Nursing Associations. In some parishes in poor districts, however, there are very few helpers, beyond one or two paid "Visitors" or Bible-women. Altogether, the number who take part in work of this kind, systematically and casually, must be large. But there are three points to which, in considering the question, the attention is chiefly drawn. First: there is little or no study or training in the administration of relief. Such study or training forms no part of the education of the clergy or non-conformist ministers. *A fortiori*, it forms no part of the education of the almoners who are subject to their direction. Next, no general principles of relief are accepted or acted upon by these administrators. They dislike being imposed upon, and they draw a marked distinction between those who are known to deceive them or are vicious or drunken, " the undeserving," and those whom they help—" the deserving." They make little or no inquiry, for effectual inquiry seems to them to be a sign of doubt, and they do not wish to seem to doubt their applicants; and their relief is most often given irregularly or at winter time, and in very small amounts. Thirdly: the great mass of the people take no part in the administration of relief. A few parishes have Relief Committees, on which members of their congregation serve. If the decision of cases is in their hands, this is a great check upon the individual almoner, and is a useful beginning of organisation. The working classes give not a little relief to their mates in connection with their Trade and Friendly Societies. There are also " Philanthropic

Societies" in several districts, supported by local tradesmen and others. But, if we set aside those who are working with parishes and chapels, as above described, and those who are in some way—as clergy or ministers—engaged in the administration of relief, few—certainly few in the poorer parts of London—have any interest in the subject or give up time to it. It is not recognised as one of the ordinary duties of a citizen, as we find it to be in some German towns—Elberfeld, Dresden, Berlin, and others. It is not a municipal duty, except in so far as it is the duty of a comparatively small number of Guardians and their Officers. On the other hand, it is a part of the duty of religious bodies who have religious aims in view, and who usually make their relief subservient to their aims. And these religious bodies themselves are actuated by conflicting motives and are often antagonistic, competing one with another for the schooling of the children in the neighbourhood. Charity in their eyes is not a central rallying point for the thought and life of the community in its earnest endeavours to help the fallen, strengthen the feeble-hearted, and lift the pauper out of degradation. It is rather a thing that shifts and changes with their religious and social differences. It is not

> An ever fixed star
> That looks on tempests and is never shaken.

Rather is it like the light of torches, carried by a hurrying crowd, which move as they move, and which flare or flicker, as the wind blows gently or in gusts, or as the torch-bearers step slowly or quickly.

Into a social world such as this, we have to bring charity organisation.

(2.) *Charity Organisation Societies.*

In England and Scotland there are about 68 Charity Organisation Societies, if we include some Societies for improving the condition of the poor, with which Charity Organisation Societies are in co-operation. There are Charity Organisation Societies in Adelaide, Melbourne and Sydney; and in America there are some 78 Societies called—some, Charity Organisation Society, some, "Associated Charities," some by other titles, but all with similar aims.

Some Charity Organisation Societies, if one may judge them from their Reports, seem rather

Investigation and Relief Societies, than Charity Organisation Societies, the distinctive feature of which is co-operation with individuals and institutions for the relief and care of cases of distress. In America, where there is no such strong parochial system as there is in England, and no Established Church, the Societies have developed a system of friendly visiting, and a plan of central registration of all cases of distress, beyond what is to be found in connection with our English Societies. In many Societies there are distinctive features, to which reference will be made later on. Generally speaking, the objects of Charity Organisation Societies are stated in similar terms, although there is considerable variation in practice. Some Societies have indeed, in the matter of relief, departed widely from sound principle, and distribute large sums in small amounts and in kind. But, generally speaking, they are a protest, and sometimes a strong and recognised protest, against relief without inquiry, untrained almsgivers, inadequacy of assistance and want of co-operation. Their object may be stated in a limited and very practical form in the following extract taken from the Manual of the London Society.

"The main object of the Society is the improvement of the condition of the poor, (1) by bringing about co-operation between the Charities and the Poor Law, and amongst the Charities; (2) by securing due investigation and fitting action in all cases; and (3) by repressing mendicity."

In London there are 40 District Committees of the Society. The area of these Committees is that of the Poor Law Unions or Parishes, but in very large Unions or Parishes there are sometimes two or more Committees. If the large population in most of these districts be taken into account, the Committees might fairly be considered as important as separate Societies. In four suburban districts—Eltham, Streatham and Tooting, Stoke Newington and Holloway, the Society has no Committees, though in the last named district, which has now a large population, a Committee is much wanted. The Society is a federation of these Committees, each of which, in order to be in union with it, must act on certain general principles and must appoint representatives on the general Council. The Honorary Secretaries and Chairmen of the Committees are *ex-officio* members of this Council. This Council and its Committees conduct the general business of the Society.

Some twenty District Committees receive grants from the Council towards their expenses of management. Some are chiefly maintained by these grants. In some instances, besides these grants, assistance is given to a Committee on the poorer parts of London by paying for a special Officer, a District Secretary, who is appointed by the Council with a view to developing organisation in districts in which it has not made progress, ensuring good "case-work," promoting co-operation, and enlisting volunteers. About £1300 a year is now spent by the Council in this way. Those who are appointed are educated men and women, who are trained for the work, and have a special interest in it, and are ready, for a comparatively small salary, to give up their whole time and thought to it. Apart from these grants and this assistance, the District Committees are financially independent. In 1887-8 the office expenses of all the District Committees amounted to £9,481, or, on an average, £237. This money is spent, apart from necessary expenditure in printing, &c., in (1) Officers and (2) Rent. It is found that, to deal properly with a large number of cases, to hear in private the tales of those in distress, and to provide accommodation for volunteers who help in the work by seeing applicants, arranging about relief, writing letters and so forth, at least three or four rooms are necessary. These rooms include a Committee-room and one that serves as a waiting-room. But the main condition which governs the question of accommodation is the necessity of hearing facts of each case in a private manner and without undue delay. Next as to Officers. The Officers in charge of the work in most districts are Honorary Secretaries —men and women, who give a very great deal of time to the work, treating it indeed in many instances as the business of their lives. Upon them the progress of the Committee very largely depends, and to their patient and unsparing labour the Society owes a full measure of thanks. There are often two, and sometimes three, Honorary Secretaries in one Committee. Often members of Committee take special departments of work, such as the accounts, or the general care of pension or loan cases. In the poorer districts, for which Honorary Secretaries able to give sufficient time to the work, cannot be found, the District Secretaries, to whom I have referred, are appointed. Sometimes, where the work is heavy, they work with and under Honorary Secretaries. The Committees also in richer districts often have paid Secretaries.

Besides Secretaries, there are in a District Office, according to the amount of the work, one or more Agents or Inquiry Officers. On these men devolve the major part of the work of inquiry. The point at which the volunteer takes up the case, is different in different districts. As a rule the applicants for relief come to the District Office. Their statements are then taken down, sometimes by the Honorary or the District Secretary, sometimes by the Agent, sometimes by members of Committee. Then follows the inquiry, made usually by the Agent or Inquiry Officer, but sometimes in part by a volunteer, in part by the paid officer. Then the case with the inquiries complete is submitted to the Committee. Formerly, the volunteers did not as a rule intervene till this stage. Now volunteers take a larger share in the work throughout. At some Committees the applicants are seen at Committee, at others care is taken that the Secretary or some member of Committee should see them before the meeting, but they do not themselves attend. Opinions differ as to which is the better plan. Personally, I prefer the latter. When a decision has been arrived at, if the case has to be visited or relief obtained, the labour of making the necessary arrangements is undertaken by the Secretary and the members of Committee. The bulk of the money required for relief is raised, as we say, "specially" for the case, from Charitable Societies and individuals. In 1887-8 the relief thus raised amounted to £18,114; loans were made amounting to £1,570; and grants from the general funds of Committee were made to the amount of £3,581. The Committees consist of members of all denominations and of all political creeds. There is no question whatever of the use of relief for any proselytising purpose. Consideration is, indeed, paid to religious differences; thus, a Committee would not think of sending the child of a Catholic to a Protestant home or *vice versâ*. But, otherwise, religious differences are, so far as the Society is concerned, set aside for the common ends of charity.

It is desired that the Committees should contain representatives of the Board of Guardians, and of all charities (including in that term

Parochial and Chapel Charities) at work in the district. In many, probably most districts, one or more members of the Board of Guardians are on the Charity Organisation Committee, and there is sometimes close co-operation with them. Generally some of the Parishes are represented; often, even if not represented, there is co-operation; in a few instances, mutual help; in many instances, a one-sided co-operation. For sometimes, it must be confessed, the clergy send cases of which they wish to be rid; sometimes they send cases, but are not ready to join in providing the required aid; and sometimes they reserve their funds for what we should consider mischievous or useless relief, and then are unable or unwilling to aid the Committee in giving effectual help to a good case. We always do the best we can for the applicant, however, whether the clergy help or refuse to help; for, when once we have taken up a case and found some plan of assisting it, we take upon ourselves the trouble of raising the relief and seeing that it is properly dealt with. The Nonconformist Chapels are seldom represented on our Committees at present. With charitable institutions our co-operation is chiefly in connection with individual cases. We have special arrangements with only one or two; but every year more is done by way of practical co-operation. In one or two districts working-men serve on the Committees. We get comparatively little help from the tradesmen class. Many members of our Committees in poor districts come from the West End; and one of the chief difficulties in the way of forming Committees really representative of these districts is that of arranging hours of meeting which will be convenient to all alike. The average attendance at a Committee would, I think, be eight or ten. There are sometimes a number of semi-detached members of Committee who are called Associates. Often the Committee is large, and the attendance of a section of its members is irregular. The size of the Committee is no index of the number of the people with which it is in co-operation, as occasion offers.

The Council of the London Society has formed for its executive work an Administrative Committee, which is elected by the Council out of members of Council, nominated by the District Committees. It consists of twenty members, fifteen thus elected and five co-opted. One of its Sub-Committees supervises the work of District Committees, and subject to the approval of the Administrative Committee, passes the estimates of annual expenditure which each Committee is required to furnish, and makes grants for the maintenance of Committees in the poorer districts. Subject to the approval of the Districts' Sub-Committee, in cases in which District Committees are unable to raise the sum required for adequate relief, *e.g.*, in cases of long illness, maintenance for a long period in a home or school, and pensions, funds are raised by the insertion of advertisements in the *Charity Organisation Review*, and in the general press. About £1,300 was thus obtained last year. In connection with another Sub-Committee, special arrangements have been made for co-operation with hospitals and for assisting District Committees in obtaining suitable convalescent and surgical aid with promptitude. Another Sub-Committee deals with emigration. Another branch of the work of the Council consists in publishing periodically a *Charities' Register and Digest* of charities and benevolent institutions by whose aid cases from the Metropolis may be dealt with; in furnishing to inquirers legitimately interested reports in regard to appeals, more particularly appeals from charitable institutions, and in registering cases of fraud and imposture, and, as far as possible, warning the public against them. Besides these branches of work, the Council, by means of Special Committees, has dealt with many questions of special importance connected with Charity Organisation, such as charity and cheap food, soup-kitchens, the dwellings of the poor, the training of the blind, the education and care of idiots, imbeciles, and harmless lunatics, voting charities, medical relief, the employment of Italian children for mendicant or immoral purposes. At the present time there is a Special Committee on the Preparation and Audit of the Accounts of Charities, and another Committee is promoting a Parliamentary inquiry into the management and common organisation of Hospitals and Dispensaries and Poor Law Infirmaries and Dispensaries in the Metropolis.[1]

On the various purposes of organisation the Council expended, in 1887-8, £4,967; the District Committees expended £10,833—in all about

---

[1] Since the above was written, the Committee on Accounts has published its report, and a Select Committee has been appointed by the House of Lords to make inquiry in regard to the Hospitals of the Metropolis.

£15,800. The relief administered by the Society in 1887-8 amounted to £26,248. In 1887-8, the District Committees dealt with (exclusive of 2,610 cases withdrawn) 24,753 cases, of which 11,322 were not assisted, while 13,431 were assisted, some in one way, very many in several ways and by several agencies. The District Committees issued in that year 11,777 Reports to inquirers about cases; the Central Office 1,302, on appeals from institutions and individuals. The number of cases dealt with by the District Committees in past years has fluctuated according to the amount of distress. It rose from 15,111 in 1878 to 21,445 in 1879. In 1881 it rose to 26,052; and during the last three years—certainly years of difficulty amongst the poorer classes—the numbers have been 26,131, 25,533, 27,363. A case represents a family. To obtain the average number of individuals, the total should be multiplied by $3\frac{1}{2}$ or 4.

From the Returns and Reports of Provincial Societies, it appears that, especially in large towns, they deal annually with many cases, but differences of methods in relief and in making up returns do not allow of any single comparative statement being made of the work of the Societies as a whole. In 1887-8 the Birmingham Society dealt with 2,414 cases; the Glasgow Society dealt with 5,098 cases, assisting 3,939; the Liverpool Central Relief and Charity Organisation Society dealt with 18,253 cases, of which 3,188 were not assisted, and 10,988 assisted— 9,340 in kind—while 1,409 received orders for work; the Society at Newcastle-on-Tyne assisted 4,910 cases, but this includes 3,857 pints of soup and bread, 443 food and 212 Dispensary letters. The New York Society, U.S.A., returns the number of cases in charge of paid and unpaid visitors in 1888 at 4,730, and in that year 15,956 new families were registered at their Central Office. This, it is stated, makes a total of 117,872 families thus registered. Apart from cases placed in charge of Churches or Societies for which relief was procured, no entry in regard to relief appears in their returns. The Boston Associated Charities, U.S.A., reported that in 1888-9 2,176 families were visited by 887 volunteer visitors, besides 2,163 cases otherwise dealt with; 7,292 families in all were in the care of the Conferences in that year. The form of these returns implies, it will be seen, a considerable difference of system and offers a marked contrast to some of the above statements of work, in which relief has so prominent a place. Of this difference we would say a word later on.

The largeness of these figures would seem to show that Charity Organisation, if it is working on the principles which it professes, must in many towns be affecting a large number of families who are on the verge of pauperism. It must also be influencing public opinion in regard to the administration of charity, and diverting to new and better ends the general current of charitable relief.

(3.) *Inquiry.*

I propose now to consider Charity Organisation and the work of Charity Organisation Societies in reference to the following points:— inquiry; almonership; relief; co-operation; and general methods of improving the condition of the people. I would then refer to some shortcomings and defects, and finally to some general indications that the methods of the Society are in harmony with certain other social forces which are tending to improve the condition of the people.

In a great city the larger proportion of applications for relief are made from strangers to strangers. It may be that the application is from an idle stranger to a busy stranger. The means of obtaining information at the disposal of a private person are usually very limited. Accordingly he may give without inquiry, because he does not know how to inquire, even if he wished to do so, or he may refuse, because he cannot inquire and cannot therefore relieve with any prospect of doing permanent good. In that case he refuses to be responsible in any way for helping the stranger out of his distress. On the other hand, if he accept the responsibility, he should at least know the facts, and according to his ability, should co-operate with others for the stranger's effectual assistance. Suppose Figaro "enfin établi dans Séville," after having "son baggage en sautoir, parcouru philosophiquement les deux Castilles, la Manche, l'Estramadure, la Sierra-Morena, l'Andalousie." Now he asks the bounty of a leading citizen with a view to setting up shop as a barber-surgeon under his sign of "Trois palettes en l'air, l'œil dans la main, *Consilio manuque*, FIGARO." How should the citizen in these days of a nicer division of labour, ascertain whether the philosophic barber did not run the gauntlet of the

CHARITY ORGANISATION. 63

police in the two Castilles, and whether, notwithstanding the good sign of his craft, which he proposes to set up, he really knows the business of either barber or surgeon and apothecary, and can turn to good account the little capital with which it is proposed to give him a start? The citizen must inquire; and unless he have a network of correspondents, he cannot. Such correspondents are Charity Organisation Societies. They will inquire one of another; and if they conclude that the said Figaro should be assisted, they will do their best, in conjunction with the said citizen and others, to give him a good start. If not—they will tell the citizen of Figaro's escapades; and no doubt Figaro will ask some one else.

Of adventurers there are many. Some establish charities and make fine profits out of the venture. Some appeal to the great men of one or both political parties, and in the shape of bounty receive no inconsiderable compensation for the services which they say that they have rendered. Some are from what we call half-sharps, men and women who combine cunning with a touch of insanity. Indeed the appeals come from people of all kinds, and are often the saddest sign of false, degraded, miserable and dependent lives. Sometimes, however, the appeal is made in a first trouble, the petitioner can be restored to independence; and sometimes continual care will work a change. But in all cases alike, inquiry—a knowledge of the facts—is necessary.

There are other cases, too, in which inquiry is necessary, but in which it is seldom so considered. A district visitor will say, " I know Mrs. B—; I should not like to make any inquiry about her." And yet she may be puzzled to know how to help her; and without inquiry, it may not be possible to learn how to do so. In spite of the casual or even regular visits of the visitor, Mrs. B. has really remained a stranger to her. Mrs. B. has kept her own counsel in regard to a large number of important matters—such, for instance, as to whether any of her relations are able to help her. She has talked to the visitor about religious matters and otherwise of matters indifferent. Without actually playing the hypocrite, she has assumed towards her a certain mental attitude—put on, so to speak, certain mental clothes—so that the visitor knows not her, but only this more or less artificial and muffled representation of her which she has allowed her to see. Yet in all these cases—indeed, in all cases—inquiry is necessary, if charity is to fulfil its object of helping the individual, and at the same time bettering the social life of the poor.

But in regard to the need of inquiry, there is a general concurrence of opinion. The churches have recognised it. The Society for St. Vincent de Paul has adopted it in principle. The official, but unpaid, almoner in the celebrated Elberfeld system is " appointed to the most important civic and honorary office, the worthy performance of which requires a large amount of active charity, and a firm sense of justice; charity to listen to the request of the poor with kindness of heart and friendliness; firmness, in order to refuse unjustifiable claims, to ascertain, after careful scrutiny, the amount of assistance necessary, and to prevent idleness and immorality being assisted and promoted by relief." A similar duty is laid on the Relieving Officer of an English Union (see above). In Charity Organisation Societies, there is usually inquiry by a paid officer, often supplemented by the visits of a volunteer. The principle then is accepted; the difficulty is to apply it, and to make it the rule and not the exception, a reality and not a mere form. Now, if, as at Elberfeld, or generally in Germany, unpaid citizens undertake the inquiry in connection with the administration of relief, it is necessary that they should work in small manageable districts, and should deal with only a few cases each. With devotion on their part, help from paid officials in regard to certain portions of the investigation, and a strict adherence to principles, we may expect from this system the best results. It puts before charitable persons the greatest inducement to join hands with the administrators of civic relief, or, at least, not to interfere with them by relieving cases which are under their care. It allows of the exercise of influence by the individual in the individual case, and thus promote the recovery from pauperism of many who would otherwise be permanently degraded. It is on these lines, but as voluntary associations, that several of the American Societies have developed their work, I understand, very successfully, and the system is being introduced into Liverpool and Glasgow.

But in very large towns the civic energy at the service of a municipal system of relief is likely to be weak. Desirous of breaking through the narrowness of parochialism and private interests, and disinclined to rely too exclusively on civic energy, the English have, in Poor Law administration, adopted the system of large areas with paid Inquiry and Relief Officers. And, if the area be large, and the number of Officers insufficient for purposes of stringent inquiry, it follows that "tests" must, in a great measure, take the place of inquiry.[1] Further, it must be added, that in some very poor districts, and in a shifting population, thorough inquiry is very difficult, and produces less result in the way of definite information than might be expected. Tests, such as the Workhouse test, have thus, in fact, become one of the means of dealing with applications for Poor Law relief in England. But they afford no absolute substitute for inquiry; and when by good administration the number of applications is

[1] Tests may be defined as offers of relief made under conditions, which the applicant, if he be not actually destitute, will consider less eligible than doing without relief altogether. They are a kind of "Hobson's choice." The decision, as to whether relief should or should not be given, is shifted from the administrator to the applicant, who, according to his own estimate of his needs and desires, settles whether he will accept or refuse.

reduced, it becomes more and more easy to make thorough investigation, the good results of which are speedily manifest.

Next, as to inquiry by trained almoners in connection with voluntary associations. In very large towns the trained almoners, with discernment, force of character, and power of influencing the weak and wayward, are rare, compared with the large number of applications that come to the notice of those who are engaged in relieving distress. If, under these circumstances, the plan of visitors with small areas, to inquire into and care for cases of distress, is introduced, it would almost certainly break down, or degenerate into a system of insufficient inquiry and "District Visiting." In large towns, therefore, it is necessary, I believe, to adopt a hybrid system of inquiry in part by paid Visitor or Inquiry Officer, who may become an expert in such work, in part by a volunteer. On this plan the maximum use may be made of capable volunteers. Many cases, however, which inquiry shows to be unsatisfactory, but which, on the method of small areas, and a distribution of a few cases to each visitor, might be raised to independence, may have to be set aside, because the strength and number of the members of the organisation cannot cope with them. In very large towns we have to create a new spirit of personal charity, as well as greater interest in civic affairs. Whatever system be adopted, however, inquiry is essential, and the volunteers should, whether in the inquiry, or in the subsequent work of assistance, be constantly brought into contact with the poor, especially in their own homes.

I quote two extracts here by way of evidence; one is taken from the Report of the Superintendent of the Out Relief Department of the Parish of Birmingham, and shows the necessity of inquiry in the administration of public relief, while it throws light on the actual administration of the Poor Law. Another extract, which I will quote later on, from the Report of a District Committee of the London Charity Organisation Society, illustrates the need of inquiry in the administration of voluntary relief.

In Birmingham the Poor Law Guardians employ what they call a " Cross Visitor."

" The Cross Visitor," the report states, " has recorded in his special report-books seven cases of imposition which he has discovered when making surprise visits during the year. Many others were detected by the joint efforts of this Officer and the Relieving Officers, but these are not included in his report. Only those cases are reported where he alone is responsible for the discovery. He also devotes special attention to all new applications for out relief, and old cases receiving relief are renewed at short intervals. The result of these frequent visits is that some cases are proved not to be destitute, others are shown to be undeserving, while many, both new and old, are found chiefly by surprise visits to have relatives liable for their maintenance, and who are able to support them. These facts had been studiously withheld until an unexpected visit was made. In many instances a son, said to be in America for years, is then discovered. It is frequently very amusing how the threads of discovery unravel themselves. Sometimes a workman's basket on a side table, which is said to have belonged to a husband who had been dead twelve years; a hat behind the door, or a stray coat on the sofa; a man washing himself in the pantry, who was a perfect stranger, and had just called in and asked if he might have this privilege; a pipe on the mantel-piece which evidently had been in use a few minutes before,

CHARITY ORGANISATION. 71

but which is said to belong to a child aged five years, who is fond of playing with such articles; or frequently the person is said to be a brother, a cousin, or some distant relative that has just called to see them. No doubt in some instances this is quite true; but in the majority it is otherwise. Only the other day one of the Relieving Officers paid a surprise visit to a widow receiving relief, when he found a man in a drunken condition without his coat or waistcoat, and before the woman could give any reason for the man's presence he exclaimed, 'What the — do you want here? I'm landlord now, and your place is outside. We get no — parish relief now.' These and other things lead to detection, and, of course, they all occur where female lodgers only are kept. In these and other ways many names disappear from the pauper roll who have been deceivers for years."

"Special cases reported by the Cross Visitor in each district:—

	1884.	1885.	1886.	1887.	1888.	
In District 1 there were	20	10	3	4	0	cases.
,, 2 ,,	6	7	6	5	0	,,
,, 3 ,,	3	3	7	4	4	,,
,, 4 ,,	14	7	9	3	2	,,
,, 5 ,,	6	2	0	0	0	,,
,, 6 ,,	0	0	0	0	1	,,

"The Relief Committees discontinued the relieving for the following reasons:—

	1884.	1885.	1886.	887.	1888.	
Cohabiting with men,	12	2	4	2	0	cases.
Drunkenness,	9	6	3	0	3	,,
Deception,	13	6	4	5	3	,,
Income sufficient,	3	10	9	5	0	,,
Widows with illegitimate children,	4	4	4	3	0	,,
Non-appearance at Relief Committee,	4	1	1	0	1	,,
Filthy homes,	4	0	0	1	0	,,

"An order for the Workhouse is made by the Relief Committees when they are satisfied that a person who is receiving out relief is not destitute or is undeserving, or is living under conditions which they cannot approve; and also upon the recommendation of the District Medical Officers when proper nursing, diet, and infirmary treatment is indispensable to recovery. There were twenty-four such orders made during the year, but two only were used."

"They are thus classified:—

Why the order was made.	No. of Orders.				
	1884.	1885.	1886.	1887.	1888.
Sufficient income to maintain family,	62	41	33	11	4
Immorality & women with illegitimate children,	5	6	11	8	2

CHARITY ORGANISATION. 73

Why the order was made.		No. of Orders.			
	1884.	1885.	1886.	1887.	1888.
Ill and having dirty homes	42	29	31	9	9
Irregular school attendance,	13	0	3	2	4
Drinking,	21	10	11	8	7
Imposture,	19	18	13	15	5
Desertion,	3	0	2	0	0
Husband in Prison,	3	0	1	0	0
Left the Parish,	1	5	0	0	0
Begging,	1	0	0	1	0
Selling Parish bread,	0	1	0	0	0

"In my previous annual reports I have described at some length flagrant cases of deception that had been detected during the year, but these cases must become fewer year by year, for as the undeserving are from time to time weeded out, the number must of necessity become smaller, and your officers' energies are restricted to what might be termed 'cases in a state of development.'"

Inquiry in connection with Charity Organisation is objected to on several grounds. It causes delay, it is said. Some delay, no doubt, must occur; some time for the inquiry must be allowed. But, at the most, it is only a delay of a few days; and, if necessary, interim relief can be given in the meanwhile. Another objection is that inquiry is made, but, if the Committee considers the case unsuitable, nothing is done. But the question whether help should or should not be given is dependent on the results of the inquiry and the possibility of giving remedial assistance. The inquiry would otherwise be purposeless. If, on the statement of the applicant, it is clear that the Committee cannot aid him, the case is generally stopped at the outset. To those who have become accustomed to expect relief without inquiry, it is vexatious. And no doubt inquiry, conducted in a purely official and unsympathetic manner, is humiliating, and seems inquisitorial. But if the general methods sketched in this paper are adopted, there need be no ground for complaint on this score. In most cases people are very ready to tell their troubles. "The petty meannesses and want of straightforwardness" of the better class of applicants, as one of our District Committees wrote,[1] "often cause far more trouble than more deliberate imposition."

"In nearly every case in which the Committee has been unsuccessful during the past year, the cause of failure has been traced to some relaxation of principles on account of what seemed to

[1] "Annual Report of the Council of the London Charity Organisation Society." 1886-7,

be exceptional features in the case. What can be more like red-tapism, it may be asked, than always to verify a man's statement as to his addresses for the two years preceding his application? A highly-recommended and very respectable tradesman, who had been in a good position and had become a bankrupt owing to the vicinity of 'stores,' was lent £15 by the Committee to open a small confectionery business, which proved a failure. Exact inquiries ought to have shown that shortly before his application he had failed in a precisely similar undertaking in another part of London. In this case only a few weeks had escaped notice between two addresses. (This applicant has, nevertheless, since got other employment, and is repaying the loan.) Sometimes inquiries have been omitted, because a case was recommended by a clergyman or some other person of position. One of the most unsatisfactory cases dealt with during the year was recommended by eleven clergymen. In a case in which the inquiry was curtailed at the special request of a doctor, the man proved dishonest, but the doctor would give no assistance in bringing him to book. There are always persons who will trade upon their respectability. The wife of a retired police-constable obtained, on an emergency, a surgical instrument for a child, for which, she said, she could not afford to pay. On being asked why she had suppressed all mention of her husband's pension of £50 a year, she became very indignant, and protested that the family were all teetotalers! A postman failed to pay 5s. which he had promised towards three weeks' expenses at Westgate-on-Sea, and complained that it was 'a queer kind of charity which expected you to pay back.' It is fortunate that these cases are exceptional, and not the rule, but each one, as it occurs, points to the conclusion that in any public institution for dealing with the difficulties of the poor, nothing but a rigid adherence to system will ensure that the right objects are attained and imposture suppressed."

As to plans of inquiry, I find, as is natural, that they are very similar. Inquiry must obviously include the following points:—Previous addresses; the present address; the names, number and ages of the family; their employments, etc.; their wages; their debts and liabilities; their relations; their claims on Friendly and other Societies; their assets; the relief which they are receiving from any quarter; how they can be permanently benefited. Further, by inquiry of Officers who are acting on behalf of the public administration of relief, of the schoolmaster, the clergy and others, or by visiting the home, the applicants' statements must be verified. Some plan of assistance, if any be feasible, will thus be evolved; and if there be fraud, it will probably come to light.

(4.) *The Almoner.*

Whatever the form of Charity Organisation that may be adopted, the aim and end of the system is to aid and train the almoner.

If we could revive the past, and out of it create the modern almoner, I think that, though much would be different, we would endow him with a large portion of the spirit of St. Francis. The true almoner is practical. He does not go to life with rules, but from life he draws his rules. The Franciscan saying was, "A man's knowledge is equal to his works." The real knowledge is the knowledge that can be worked into life. Poverty to the Franciscan was the condition of sharing in the life of others. To him the injunction was absolute. His monastery was to be no better than the poor man's hovel;

like his master he would eat out of the same dish as a leper. The learning of books he set aside for the learning of life; and so, almost in spite of himself, he became skilled in philosophy and medicine, in the use of thought and speech, in knowledge and in the application of knowledge. He had the simple rule of the triple vow, as the key which was to unlock life to him, and for the rest—" the brothers of that time having the first fruits of the spirit, were content not with human constitutions, but the affections of a free devotion—content with the rule and very few other regulations." There was the utmost adaptability on the part of the Franciscan. He was no priest, but a layman under a religious vow. He was independent in spirit, and attacked with a cheerful hopefulness the social problem of the day—the misery, squalor and vice of a mediæval city, by methods of his own devising. He was original. He thought out the old problem afresh for himself; and consequently he attacked it with the vigour and directness of originality. Suppose an alliance between this devotion, courage and simplicity, and the spirit of citizenship or associated charity, as, trying to acquire form and organisation, it may now be seen in a modern city, and we have, I think, a vivid picture of what the almoner should be.

Of those who have in our time given a new turn to thought in this direction, Miss Octavia Hill, has, I think, had the most influence. To her, as much as to any, is due the general acceptance of the doctrine of the responsibility of charity, as a personal obligation; and in America certainly her papers have contributed very much towards the foundation of the special methods of Charity Organisation, which have there sprung up. In evidence of this I cannot do better than make an extract taken from an address of Miss Hill's and quoted in "The Work of Volunteer Visitors of the Associated Charities among the Poor," by Mr. R. Treat Paine, President of the Associated Charities of Boston.[1]

"I hope you will notice that I have dwelt on the need of restraining yourselves from almsgiving on the sole ground that such restraint is the only true mercy to the poor themselves. I have no desire to protect the purses of the rich,

[1] Read at the Social Science Conference at Saratoga, September, 1880.

no hard feeling to the poor. I am thinking continually and only of what is really kindest to them—kindest in the long run, certainly, but still kindest. I think small doles unkind to them, though they bring a momentary smile to their faces. First of all, I think they make them really poorer. Then I think they degrade them and make them less independent. Thirdly, I think they destroy the possibility of really good relations between you and them. Surely when you go among them, you have better things to do for them than to give them half-crowns. You want to know them—to enter into their lives, their thoughts; and let them enter into some of your brightness; to make their lives a little fuller, a little gladder. You who know so much more than they, might help them so much at important crises of their lives . . . . . but I do believe the poor *have* lessons to teach us of patience, vigour and content, which are of great value to us. We shall learn them instinctively if we are among them as we ought to be, as friends. It is this side of your relation to them, that of being their friends, which has given all the value to your work as District Visitors: it has been because you have been friends—and in as far as you have been friends—that the relation between you has been happy and good."

This view led naturally to an organisation of charity on the basis of "Friendly Visiting." A clause in the list of objects of the Boston Associated Charities indicates this. It is thus expressed :—

"To send to each poor family, under the advice of a district conference, a friendly visitor."

The "Friendly Visiting" takes the place of "District Visiting," such as is usually carried on in connection with the parish and church organisation in England. Instead of a district being assigned to a visitor, the visitor is asked to befriend some one or more families. Boston has a population of about 250,000 inhabitants. The Associated Charities have organised 14 districts in it, each with its Conference. The object of the Conference is "to organise charity, so that the best thing may be done to insure the permanent welfare of the poor." At the Conferences are discussed plans of improving the condition of the poor in the district, and methods of dealing with individual cases. The inquiry in regard to the latter is made by a paid

F

visitor; and attached to most Conferences there is a small Executive Committee whose duty it is to arrange the work for the Conference, and to study each case, so as to assign it judiciously to the best visitor, or, if necessary, to secure for it from other sources the needful help. Relief on this plan falls into the back-ground. Other bodies give it, with the knowledge of the Associated Charities, but direct. The cases are not, as in most Charity Organisation Societies, decided, and then, unless there is some special reason for keeping touch of them, allowed to slip out of sight. They remain in the hands of the visitors permanently, unless a change of visitor is desirable; and the object of the Associated Charities is to create a charitable friendship between the family and visitor—a friendship which may always be available in case of need. But the visitor gives no relief; he is a friend only, advising and persuading. The work, like that at Elberfeld, is done in great detail. Its success depends on the visitor's strength of character. Some will succeed where others fail. Hard cases, which may be found too hard by some, others may be able to influence after a time by patience and tact. In the Annual

Returns of the Associated Charities there are entries of the numbers influenced to become thrifty, to give up intemperance, and so forth— entries which show in what direction the Society wishes to advance, whatever be the actual inequality of work in different Conferences.

The power to befriend others in this way is a gift which all do not possess. The question is how to turn it to account wherever it is found. The method of Associated Charity probably gives it the best scope. Every type of case also, it should be added, can be dealt with on this plan —if the visitor be forthcoming, not only those in which relief by itself is all that is required, or in which it is clear that good will immediately result from this or that definite plan of help.

In London any general approach to a system of this kind is a far-off vision; but we think that on our present methods we are influencing public opinion and thus organising charity, so that very slowly and by degrees, in all cases in which friendly intervention is necessary, there may be a skilled and kindly almoner, who may, as far as possible, remove the causes of distress. Meantime every year the number of those who take an active personal share in our work is larger; and more thought is given to training the almoner. There is, however, amongst us a certain want of faith in the strength of individual effort—a want of faith partly due to the difficulties which are incidental to work of this kind in a very large town; and only very slowly will it be trusted as it should be.

As to training, probably the best training is the experience that comes of failure when head and heart have done their best, and there is no room for blame. But the training should be methodic. New members should acquire at least an elementary knowledge of the history and principles of the administration of relief, and of its relation to social life and economics. But their chief work should be to learn what are the obligations, possibilities and limits of charity. They should visit, make inquiries, take charge of cases—such as pension cases, and after a time take down applications. All, however, should, as far as possible, be done under supervision. Whether this part of the work be successful or not, will depend chiefly on the Honorary or District Secretary.

The first condition of a widespread system of Friendly Visitors or Almoners, is a general acceptance by the public of the responsibility of personal charity. As this view spreads, all the qualities that go to make up an earnest and ordered individual charity, will be developed— the self-restraint, the firmness of purpose, the fulness of resource, the definiteness and the educational force of the newer charity, and the unutterable gentleness, the sympathy, and the strong religious impulse and idealism of the older.

I do not quote instances; but many might be quoted to show the results of individual work done in this spirit.

(5.) *Relief.*

A further principle in Charity Organisation is, that all decisions in regard to relief should not only be made after inquiry, but in Committee. A Committee is the first step towards co-operation. It gives many an opportunity of working together without distinction of class or creed. It educates the almoner. It leads to the proper allotment of the common work. It prevents irregular and impulsive giving, and keeps performance to a higher standard than it would reach if left to itself.

Next, as has been shown, the tendency of organisation is towards *obtaining* and not giving the relief required for the individual case of distress. This method rouses interest, and draws as many institutions and private persons as possible into co-operation. It also leads a Committee to consider a case on its merits, irrespective of the question whether or not it has any relief funds at hand, or at its immediate disposal. In this way, too, it is likely that doles will be avoided, and a plan of relief devised, which outsiders, who are asked to help, will recognise as fitting and reasonable. The Committee will thus do its work under a kind of constraint to organise charity.

By way of illustrating the methods of relief, I would refer to two classes of cases, pension cases and "out-of-work" cases.

In pension cases, with the object of promoting self-dependence among the poor, we obtain relief when the following conditions are fulfilled:—

>   (1) There must be evidence of good character, of thrift, and of reasonable efforts to provide for the future.
>   (2) There must be a medical certificate

as to the applicant's general health and capacity for work.

(3) Unless there be exceptional circumstances, no application for a pension is entertained for any person under 60 years of age.

(4) No pension is approved which will not enable the recipient to live decently and in moderate comfort.

(5) No application for a pension is approved, unless the relations legally or morally liable will undertake to give reasonable assistance.

(6) No pensions are given in supplementation of out-door relief.

(7) The pensions are allowances renewable from time to time—as a rule every six months, subject to a careful report from a visitor. The allowances are paid by almoners weekly at the homes of the recipients.

Then as to "out-of-work" cases. By these I mean cases of builders, painters and others, in which the head of the family is ordinarily out of work for some time every winter. Not so much want of work as want of seasonable weather for work is the cause of distress. In these cases we usually refuse relief, unless there is a clear prospect of employment. But if a visitor will act on the plan of influencing the family to save during the summer for the winter's distress, a permanent cure may be accomplished. This would seem to us the best plan. Not infrequently we relieve conditionally on the head of a family joining a Friendly Society. Sometimes we help indirectly by enabling a daughter to take service, with the assistance of the Metropolitan Association for Befriending Young Servants. Relief by work may be suitable in cases of vagrants and wayfarers; but though as a test it may answer, especially at first, many are likely to look upon it as a source of income winter after winter, and it will not lead them to meet their difficulties by the only sufficient method—thrift. It is difficult also to use work, especially if large numbers are employed, as a medium for the reformation of character. Possibly with single men, under very close supervision, it may be serviceable for this purpose. On the whole, however, we should not, for many reasons, intervene by schemes of providing work, unless there were very exceptional distress.

CHARITY ORGANISATION. 89

(6.) *Co-operation.*

Co-operation is the counterpart of individual work. It is the necessary supplement of it. A case may have many needs. From one quarter relief is obtained from a hospital, from another a loan is procured, from a third assistance for a child. A Committee must, therefore, be a centre of co-operation. The co-operation will not, as a rule, be the result of some pre-arranged agreement, but will take place upon the case, as it occurs. With some Societies the Society in London is in close co-operation—with some Hospitals, with the Society for the Relief of Distress, with the Association for Befriending Young Servants, with the Homes for Aged Poor. With many it co-operates casually.

Only by co-operation is it possible to prevent the interference of many almoners from different Churches or Societies in one case, to secure proper care and aid for each case, to insure that those who should not be helped, are not helped. Here I will only refer to co-operation with the Poor Law Guardians.

The reform of out-door relief in Whitechapel, St. George-in-the-East and Stepney has been carried out in co-operation with charity. It should be a duty of charity to stop and deal with all cases of distress in which pauperism can be prevented, and also to "take off the rates" all such cases. Co-operation with the Charity Organisation Society for this purpose is in force in connection with some nine or ten of the Boards of Guardians in London. In all Unions there is an interchange of information.

In his evidence before the Select Committee of the House of Lords (1888), Mr. Vallance, the Clerk of the Whitechapel Union, to which we have already referred, made a statement on this question, which will put the plan of co-operation fully before you.

"Up to 1870," he says, "the system may be said to have been that of meeting our apparent existing circumstances of need by small doles of out-door relief; the in-door establishments—at that time consisting of a mixed workhouse for the adult sick and healthy poor, and a separate school at Forest Gate—being reserved for the destitute poor who voluntarily sought refuge in them. Able-bodied men who applied for relief on account of want of employment were set to work under the Out-door Relief Regulation Order, and, in return for such work, were afforded out-door relief in money and kind. Under this system, the administration was periodically subjected to great pressure, so much so, that the aid of the police had, not unfrequently, to be invoked to restrain disorder, and afford necessary protection to officers and property. Police protection was even at times required for the Guardians during their administration of relief. The experience of the winter of 1869-70, however, was such as to lead the Guardians to review their position and earnestly to aim at reforming a system which was felt to be fostering pauperism and encouraging idleness, improvidence, and imposture, whilst the 'relief' in no true sense helped the poor. It was seen that voluntary charity largely consisted of indiscriminate almsgiving, that it accepted no definite obligation as distinct from the function of Poor Law relief, that the Poor Law was relied upon to supplement private benevolence, that the almsgivers too frequently were the advocates of the poor in their demands upon the public rates; and that both Poor Law and charity were engaged in the relief of distress, much of which a thoughtless benevolence and a lax relief administration had created. This condition of things the Guardians resolved to amend. Looking forward to the ultimate possibility of laying down a broad distinction between 'legal relief' and 'charitable aid,' and of interpreting the former as relief in the workhouse or other institution for the actually destitute, and the latter as personal sympathy and helpful charity, they began by gradually restricting out-door relief in 'out-of-work' cases. . . Thus, the labour-yard was in the course of the year (1870) closed, and it has not since been re-opened. In this process of restriction it was found that about one in ten of those who were offered in-door, in place of out-door relief, entered the workhouse, and they, in turn, gradually withdrew themselves, so that eventually the in-door pauperism resumed its normal condition. . .

. "At present, when the head of the family is sick, by reason of the perfect understanding which exists between the Guardians and the Charity Organisation Society, and indeed workers for the poor generally, the Guardians are enabled to say to the sick man, if he is not in a Benefit Club, that he will be received into the Infirmary. The Infirmary now is a separate building under medical administration, equal, it may be said, to a general hospital. By admitting the man to the Infirmary, we take security for his early recovery, as well as for his early entrance into the labour market again. With regard to his family, as a rule, where they have been struggling, and are really deserving, there is no difficulty whatever in finding charity available at once; but otherwise, we admit part of the family with him. We have never found a difficulty. The relieving officers have always been instructed to be on the alert lest charity should fail in its duty of looking after the family of a man in the Infirmary; but we have not found a case in which it has been necessary to interpose with relief in kind."

. . . .

As to widows : "A widow with dependent children is first referred to the Charity Organisation Society, the relieving officer being authorised to meet any circumstances of urgent necessity by relief in kind. In some cases, the Society may succeed in introducing the widow to service, or employment; or may, by the purchase of a mangle or sewing machine, afford her the means of achieving independence, or—succeeding in part only—the Society may refer the case back to the Guardians with a request that one or more children may be admitted into the district school. It should also be stated that 36 poor widows are employed in the Infirmary as washers and scrubbers at weekly wages."

At Oxford the co-operation between the Guardians and the Charity Organisation Society is very close. As a result, there has been a steady decrease in the number of applications for relief from the Guardians. In 1870 they were 739, in 1887, 321. And there has been simultaneously an increase in the sums put by in the Post Office Savings, from £75,086 in 1870, to £181,980 in 1886, while the members of the local Provident Dispensary, who numbered 3,500 in 1880, in 1887 numbered 6,117. The Oxford Society endeavours to take off the hands of the Guardians all persons who ought not to be receiving Poor Law relief. They raise pensions in 59 cases. At Cambridge, between October 1885 and October 1888, 131 cases were referred to the Charity Organisation Society by the Guardians, and for them relief was provided amounting to £133, besides four pensions amounting to £27 6s. a year. The co-operation between the Society and the Guardians varies greatly in different towns. In some it is but little developed. In many there has been a decrease in out-door relief; but the influence of the Society, as at Liverpool, is shown "rather in the diminution of the indiscriminate relief which formerly prevailed, and the prevalence of a sounder public opinion as to the bad effect of such relief upon the poor," than by any direct result that can be numerically stated. And here, as well as in other places, there is communication with the Guardians; and cases that seem unsuitable for Poor Law relief, are referred to the Charity Organisation Society and dealt with by them.

In the administration of relief by the parochial clergy, the most satisfactory form of co-operation, if the clergy have a Relief Committee, is obtained by mutual representation, so that a representative of the Charity Organisation Committee attends the Relief Committee, and a representative of the Relief Committee attends the Charity Organisation Committee. This, as yet, is rare. But towards the creation of some such organisation, the preliminary steps, perhaps, are now being taken. The Charity Organisation movement has already influenced public opinion very widely, and many of the more thoughtful clergy have been led to modify and improve their system of parochial relief.

In Liverpool a system of central collection of the funds of all local charitable institutions has been instituted—a very convenient method of financial co-operation. In 1887-8, £27,431 was thus received and collected from 85 of the local charities at a small percentage as the charge for collection.

(7.) *General Methods.*

A good administration of relief promotes indirectly many general methods of improving the condition of the people. It clears the ground for activity in other directions. To some of these I have referred in the course of this paper. In Manchester a District Provident Society, an old established Society, whose methods are in many ways the same as those of a Charity Organisation Society, has done most useful work by establishing nine Provident Dispensaries, which in 1888 had 18,981 members. It has also a Savings Bank department worked by visitors who have charge of districts for the purpose of collecting savings. In 1888 the deposits amounted to £2,851. A similar plan is adopted by the Birkenhead Society. In London there is a Metropolitan Provident Medical Association initiated some years ago by the Charity Organisation Society, but entirely independent of it. It has about 30,000 contributing members. Many other Societies might be mentioned in which persons who share the views of the Charity Organisation Society take an active part, and try to improve the condition of the people in the general relations of life.

(8.) *Objections to Charity Organisation.*

Especially in connection with inquiry I have mentioned several objections to the Charity Organisation Society. Of course all the world over objections are raised to the best local forms of organisation in this department. This is natural. Each one would do what he wills with his own—with the money and the time which he would set aside for purposes of charity. Even though the work of charity is essentially co-operative, there is required of him an effort to make common cause in it with others, unless under attractive and large-hearted leadership. In this plight his unwillingness, or, perhaps, his indifference, may find vent in objections, which—if they be well-grounded—can only be removed by co-operation on his part and that of others. Each added worker, if he have patience to qualify himself for his work, strengthens a truly broad-based organisation, and helps to remove the faults and imperfections which suggest objections. I will, however, give a point to much vague criticism and put into a definite form charges which are often rather felt than publicly avowed. I would formulate the criticism as follows.

" Practically, there is a large class of cases which the Charity Organisation Society cannot relieve. They are not Poor Law cases: they will not apply to the relieving officer. They are in distress, possibly even starving, but by no plan of relief can they be adequately assisted. They may be 'left to the Poor Law,' but that is not a treatment of the case, it is a phrase for ignoring it. True, an individual visitor constantly looking after the case might do much, something at any rate; but that granted, where is the visitor? The syste. '˷ ːks down unless the visitors, in comparison with the   are many, and trained. You are trying to create such a system. But without smaller areas, local help, and many conditions wanting in London for this and most other purposes, you cannot. Thus it is a question practically of either giving or refusing relief. I give my meals and other relief; you refuse. Your refusal is not a lesson in thrift; it does not necessarily help to improve the condition of the applicant, or of applicants in general. Probably it does no such thing. And my gift, perhaps, does a little harm; but it may prevent a person from starving; and out of mere sympathy with the miserable condition of the poor, one must do something," &c., &c.

To this criticism the answer is, that experience has amply shown the evil results of irregular and aimless relief upon the character of recipients; that to refuse, and to do no more, is better than to give, when to give, and to do no more, must, in all probability, do harm; that the good administration of charitable relief depends upon trained individual work, and that though it may take a long time to create an administration on these lines, good results can be expected only from this method; that it is better therefore to work for this, than to continue to relieve cases in a way which must inevitably make the formation of a better administration more difficult.

We cannot have the benefit of a complete edifice while we are still engaged on the building of it. There is a criticism incident to change, that can only be met by further and further change—until there be created a combination, far more perfect than any that at present exist, of the religious spirit of charity with a citizenship intent on the fulfilment of social duty. At present there is a fixed suspicion in the minds of many that co-operation is not advantageous. They do not believe in the responsibilities of personal charity or in its power combined with organisation to promote any great social change. They argue, like the Chinese in regard to the Yangtze-kiang river, which Captain Little is desirous of ascending in his steamer: the immortal gods, if they had intended that steamers should navigate it, would not in the midst of it have set huge rocks. The ways of nature are, they would say, not in favour of common help and united purposes, but in favour of separate action, sectarianism, competition, independence. How can energies so divergent, as those that find their satisfaction under the name of charity, be in any degree harmonised? In a community in which there are such obstacles, plainly, Charity

Organisation was never intended to exist. If it be foolish enough to try the passage, it must strike on the rocks and sink. It is not of us. It is not Chinese. It has no sanctions. It should not be. Against such arguments there is no argument except action—to steam up stream cautiously and steadily in spite of them.[1]

We think, however, that whatever form Charity Organisation may take in the future, the current sets our way. In the last fifty years there has been great progress in the condition of the people; the people are better and better able to provide for themselves. And as this is so, they should be better and better able to take part in such a method of administration as we suggest. Our administration of relief, so far as we can judge, is in harmony with the main lines of social development. The great mass of the people are continually raising themselves above the pressure of want by means which directly or

---

[1] Alas for my metaphor, Capt. Little's steamer never went up the Upper Yangtze. It was sold. Yet it served its purpose. It put the issue of the enforcement of the Chefoo Convention, by which the right to navigate the Yangtze was ceded to the English, in a concrete form, and the river has now been thrown open and Chungking made a "treaty port." So my metaphor may well remain.

indirectly we are trying to promote. In 1872 there were about 7,732,000 Members of Friendly Societies. In 1887 there were 14,175,000; and the funds of these Societies amounted to £24,120,000. The co-operative movement has grown steadily. At the end of 1888 there were 1,464 Co-operative Societies in the Kingdom, with a total membership of 992,428. Their share capital, apart from loans and reserve funds, was £10,393,394; and (not to give too many figures) goods were sold during the year to the amount of £36,735,145, and realised a net profit of £3,414,487. The history of another voluntary commercial association in London is significant. I refer to the National Penny Bank. It was established in 1875 by Mr. G. C. T. Bartley, M.P. Share Capital amounting to £12,000, afterwards increased to £25,000 was collected; and it was arranged that all the expenses should be paid out of this capital, so that if the venture failed, the depositors should lose nothing. There are now 13 branches, most of them open for parts of the day only. There are 70,000 depositors, and the number of transactions is now in the course of the year as much as a seventh of the total transactions of the Post Office with its 5,000 to 6,000 branches.

The poorest pay into the bank. In one year 38 per cent. of the deposits were found to be under one shilling. Three per cent. interest is allowed on complete pounds for complete months. The average amount held for each depositor is £8. All sums up to £10 are paid at call. The transactions are private, and the management is that of a business institution conducted in such a way as to meet the actual wants of customers. The total deposits with interest to 31 Dec., 1888, amounted to £2,826,453; and five per cent. was paid to shareholders. This is the result of business capacity in sheer competition with the state system of Post Office Savings Banks. But at these Savings Banks, too, there has also been a slow but continuous increase in deposits. In 1869 and in 1879, years I have already referred to, there was a decrease; but otherwise there has, in general, been a gradual increase. The total amounted in 1887 to £6,871,807. Trades Unionism has grown stronger also, and in the bad years at the beginning of the present decade kept many a skilled artisan from want. Mr. Giffen[1] has shown that "the estimate of 50 to 100 per cent., as the average improvement of the

---

[1] Journal of Statistical Society, March, 1886.

money wages of the working classes, is not only not excessive, but under the mark;" and there is improvement in the wages of all kinds of labour. We may take, too, other tests. We shall find that committals for trial have fallen from 20,091, in 1868, to 13,292, in 1887; and if we may trust statisticians, there are indications that there is a change in the old order of things in regard to the number of marriages—a change which may tend to quiet some of those who are anxious about "over-population." Formerly the marriage rate rose with a fall in wheat; but during the last few years this has not been the case, and it is suggested that "the standard of living has been very considerably raised, and mere sufficiency of food is no longer held to be an adequate justification of marriage." Marriages also under 21 years of age are on the decrease.

If these statements be correct—and they touch life at several different points—may we not argue that we are working "with nature," and not in an arbitrary and unreasonable manner, and that these bare figures are an indirect witness to the correctness of the methods of relief advocated in this paper? The principles we adopt are just those which the people themselves are adopting for their own security from distress.

Conclusion.

I have chronicled my conclusions in the course of this paper, but, perhaps, it will be best to set them down very shortly.

We believe in charity and in relief as its mere instrument—in itself but little. This is a new protest against the old argument, that the cause of happiness was in external goods—"which would be as if anyone should suppose that the playing well upon the lyre was owing to the instrument and not to the art." We believe in the art of charity.

Sometimes mere material relief may be enough, but if relief abound and overflow the measure of influence that should contain it, it runs to waste —it increases pauperism. With some limitations it may be broadly stated that the influence fund of the community is the true measure of its useful relief.

The usefulness of charitable institutions is increased, their injurious tendencies checked, if there be an organisation of charity, for an organisation of charity implies methods that lead to thoroughness in the care of the unfortunate and afflicted.

The methods of Charity Organisation are individual work and co-operation, aided by inquiry and, as far as possible, adequacy of assistance.

To us it seems that charity is both the "deepest conception of religion, the motive and sustaining force of an ideal community," and the "spirit of citizenship which would aim at making the citizens 'not merely live, but live well.'" To us organisation is the endeavour "to make the part instrumental to the good of the whole; to give it definiteness of function, and to adjust it to the due development of the whole. Separate and unorganised, it is," we think, "injurious; combined and organised, it is serviceable." To us "the ideas of charity and organisation are akin. The constant consideration for others which the one represents as a motive, the other represents as an actual force." The source of what strength we may have is charity: our armour and our weapons are organisation.

THE END.

Cowan & Co., Limited, Printers, Perth.

www.ingramcontent.com/pod-product-compliance
Lightning Source LLC
Chambersburg PA
CBHW020141170426
43199CB00010B/833